Illustrator
Victoria Ponikvar

Editor
Jennifer Overend Prior, M. Ed.

Editorial Project Manager
Ina Massler Levin, M.A.

Editor-in-Chief
Sharon Coan, M.S. Ed.

Art Director
Elayne Roberts

Art Coordination Assistant
Cheri Macoubrie Wilson

Cover Artist
Sue Fullam
Jose L. Tapia

Product Manager
Phil Garcia

Imaging
James Edward Grace
Ralph Olmedo, Jr.

Publishers
Rachelle Cracchiolo, M.S. Ed.
Mary Dupuy Smith, M.S. Ed.

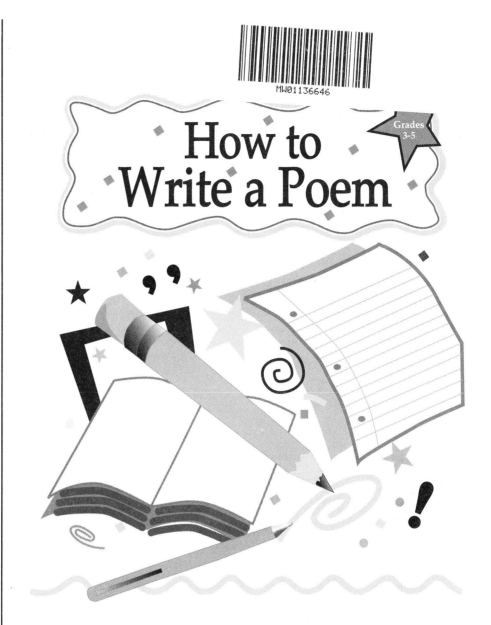

How to Write a Poem

Grades 3-5

Author

Kathleen Christopher Null

Teacher Created Materials, Inc.
6421 Industry Way
Westminster, CA 92683
www.teachercreated.com
©*1998 Teacher Created Materials, Inc.*
Reprinted, 2001, a
Made in U.S.A.
ISBN-1-57690-331-1

Table of Contents

Introduction

Some students moan and groan at the mere mention of poetry. This book will enable you to teach your students that poetry is fun and creative. The first few sections are full of ideas to assist you in introducing poetry to your students. You will find guidance in reading, appreciating, and writing poetry. The definitions will help you and your students understand some of the details of the craft of poetry. You may wish to make copies of the definitions available to your students, post them in a writing center, or simply have them handy for student questions.

The Shapes That Poetry Takes is a section that summarizes several forms of poetry. Many of these forms will be introduced to your students in the form of activities in other sections. If you wish to try other forms that are listed in this section, there is enough of an explanation to get you started.

Included is a *Warming Up with Creative Activities* section. Writers need to warm up their creative muscles just as athletes warm up before strenuous activity. There are three activities in this section: a drawing exercise, an exercise that combines feelings with similes, and a journal activity designed to increase a writer's awareness of the present moments. Each of these activities is a common exercise for poets, both present and future.

You will find a section titled, *The Poetry Tool Box*, which should be helpful in teaching some basic poetic literary tools that will increase student confidence in all forms of writing. Two sections follow that offer students the opportunity to try many different kinds of poetry, both common and not-so-common.

The book concludes with a couple of unusual poem ideas which could easily be used as creative warm ups. The class poetry magazine activity could be a culminating activity after you have completed a poetry writing or creative writing unit.

Finally, you will find a *Poetry Writing Checklist* at the end of the book. This will be useful when writing a final draft, creating a poetry magazine, or even when beginning to write.

The use of this book to supplement your own good ideas will enable you to inspire your students to achieve a greater appreciation of poetry. The activities are designed to ensure a successful experience with poetry. At the completion of several activities, your students will have not only an increased awareness of the power and joy of language but also increased self-esteem as they are able to say, "I wrote that!"

What Is Poetry?

According to the poet Marianne Moore, poems are "imaginary gardens with real toads in them." It takes imagination just to describe poetry. A poem is an "imaginary garden" because it is a creation of the poet's imagination, and because it also comes from the poet's experiences in real life, it has "real toads," too.

Poetry is all around you. It's in the jingles of jump-rope chants, television commercials, and the words of songs you like. Poetry is popular because it is fun, interesting and it's a different way to communicate ideas and feelings. Poetry comes in all shapes and sizes. Nearly any topic, mood, or feeling can be expressed in a poem. One student wanted to write about seeing deer in a canyon. She could have described them in a paragraph or written a research report on deer. She decided that a poem would be the best way for her to describe the experience. This is the poem she wrote:

A Doe and Her Fawns

I was hot, dusty, thirsty,
Coming down the trail,
The sun blinding,
When I came
To a shady canyon valley.

As my eyes adjusted
To shade and green,
Trees and creek . . .
I saw the doe.

She watched me
And concluding I was
A friend,
Bent to munch the
Short grasses.

Then I heard frolic
Up the valley wall.
The doe stood tall
And glanced my way.

Down leapt a spotted fawn,
Prancing and leaping
Joyfully dancing
To his mother's side
Where she nudged him close.

Then she looked up,
Her neck straining,
Her ears alert,
And when I looked
I saw the other.

Prancing, dancing, leaping
And playing
The other fawn oblivious to rules,
Danger, the coming darkness,
Was taken by surprise.

The doe sprang up the wall
And with a nip and a nudge
Guided her fawn back to
The safety of the valley floor.

Then looking at me
As if to say,
"What's a mother to do?"
Herded her contrite children
Through the valley's opening
Back to home
In the setting sun,

And so did I.

How to Read a Poem

If you want to write poems that you and others will enjoy reading, you will need to strengthen your "poetic ear." When you have a poetic ear, you can enjoy and appreciate reading and writing poetry. To strengthen your poetic ear, you need to read lots of poetry and write it, too.

Here is a very famous poem by American poet, Robert Frost. Read this poem, and other poems, by following the list of directions at the bottom of the page. After you've done this with a few poems, you will start to notice that your poetic ear is getting stronger.

Stopping by Woods on a Snowy Evening

Whose woods these are I think I know.
His house is in the village though;
He will not see me stopping here
To watch his woods fill up with snow.
My little horse must think it queer
To stop without a farmhouse near
Between the woods and frozen lake
The darkest evening of the year.
He gives his harness bells a shake
To ask if there is some mistake.
The only other sound's the sweep
Of easy wind and downy flake.
The woods are lovely, dark and deep
But I have promises to keep,
And miles to go before I sleep,
And miles to go before I sleep.

First, read the poem carefully all the way through. Next, read the poem aloud. When you read a poem, pay more attention to the punctuation than to the ends of lines. If there is no punctuation, go right to the next line as you read just as you would for a sentence in a story. Listen to it as you read.

Extension: Write this poem on a piece of art paper and illustrate it. Choose several poems you like and write them in a poetry journal where you can collect your favorites.

How to Write a Poem

To Write a Poem, Take These Basic Steps:

1. Choose a Subject

Just about any subject or idea will work. As you read more poetry, you will discover that poems have been written on just about every topic imaginable. It's a good idea to choose a subject that is familiar to you. Good subjects might be your pet, a family member, how you felt about an experience or event, a dream you had, or even what you see from the window of your room.

Here are a few ideas to get your imagination in gear:

Think about a subject that is very important to you. Maybe it's baseball, clean air, world peace, or new shoes. If it's important to you, it will make a good poem because you will put energy and feeling into it. Think of some subjects that are often overlooked, such as a far corner of the garage, an old toy, or even your elbow. Things we don't pay much attention to often make good poem subjects.

Think of an event in your life and write your feelings about it. It could be a death in the family, a broken arm, a flight on an airplane, or visiting a faraway relative. Remember your senses when you think of topics for poems. You could write a poem about the sound of a dripping faucet at night, the smell of your dog coming in from the rain, or the sight of the sky after a storm.

2. Prepare to Write

You may want to let your idea "incubate." Incubation is a word many writers use for prewriting. During this time, think about your topic, add to it and think of other things that are related to your topic and what it is that you want to say about it. Ask yourself "what if..." questions such as "What if my elbow got stuck?", or "What if I had three elbows on each arm?", or "What if my old teddy bear started to talk? Would he tell me about everything I did as a baby?"

3. Write the Poem

Once you have lots of ideas and notes, it's time to get your poem on paper. Some poets write their poems just once and never change them. This doesn't always happen, though, and when it does, the poet has probably spent a lot of time thinking about the poem ahead of time. Usually poems are written just like anything else that is written. There are scratch-outs, mess-ups, and changes made until it is finished. Polish it as much as you can, avoiding imitation of another poet or person. Some of the best things about poetry are that it is imperfect and individual. You can structure your poem any way you want. It can have stanzas (like paragraphs, see page 9), rhyme, or it can be free verse (see page 30). It's up to you. But don't be surprised if your poem takes shape as you are writing it.

     6

Definitions

Use these definitions to help explain various terms associated with poetry. While all of them may not be used at beginning levels, they may prove useful for those who need more challenge.

alliteration— the repetition of the beginning sound or letter in two or more words in a line of verse such as "dappled doggies dash," "bouncy bunnies," "careening cars crashing," etc.

assonance— the repetition of a vowel sound, in two or more words such as "Till the shining scythes went far and wide." (Robert Louis Stevenson)

consonance— the repetition of consonant sounds anywhere in a word (not just at the beginning as in alliteration) in a line of verse for example, "As Tommy Snooks/ and Bessy Brooks/ Were walking/ out one Sunday." (nursery rhyme)

couplet— two lines of poetry that rhyme and usually contain one complete idea

end rhyme— (also called external rhyme) when there is a rhyming of words at the ends of two or more lines of a poem, for example, "Humpty Dumpty sat on a wall,/Humpty Dumpty had a great fall."

foot— a unit of meter, iambic, anapestic, trochaic, dactylic, or spondaic (see meter). A group of two or three syllables is called a poetic foot.

internal rhyme— rhyming of words within a line of poetry, for example, "Jack Sprat could eat no fat."

metaphor— compares two different things as if they are the same, without using comparison words such as "like" or "as"; for example, "The moon is a white Frisbee floating over the mountain."

meter— a pattern of stressed and unstressed (or accented and unaccented) syllables in a line of poetry. For instance, in the word "window" the first syllable is stressed and the second syllable is unstressed. In the word "casino," only the second syllable is stressed. Here are some examples of the various types of meter in poetry:

iambic: anew, goodbye, surprise, go home
trochaic: doorknob, teaspoon, hangnail, jumpstart
dactylic: angel food, talk to me, rabbit's foot, Saturday
anapestic: cigarette, resurrect, disinfect, creamy soup, big blue book
amphibrachic: tremendous, courageous, humongous, terrific, the palace, the right way
spondaic: heartburn, big top, red house, cold fish, run down
pyrrhic: in a, so he, with it, with the, and the

Definitions *(cont.)*

onomatopoeia— a word that mimics the sound it represents; words such as *buzz, swish, zip, growl, hiss, gulp, zigzag, slither*

quatrain— a four-line stanza (see *stanza*) of four rhymed lines, rhyme scheme of various forms such as a-a-a-a, a-b-a-b, a-b-b-a, a-b-b-a, a-a-b-b, a-b-c-d

repetition— repeating a word, phrase, or sounds to add emphasis or rhythm   Probably the best example of repetition would be the lines from Edgar Allan Poe's, "The Raven." "While I nodded, nearly napping, suddenly there came a tapping, as of someone gently rapping rapping, at my chamber door."

rhyme— two or more words with the same or similar sounds.

rhyme scheme— a pattern of rhyme in a poem. For instance, if it is a quatrain and the first and the third lines rhyme, it has the pattern of a-b-a-b. If all four lines rhyme with each other, it has a rhyme scheme of a-a-a-a. If the second and fourth lines rhyme, the pattern is a-b-c-b.

simile— comparison of two different things using comparing words such as "like" or "as" An example is "I'm as hungry as a bear."

stanza— a division or section of a poem named for the quantity of lines it contains; for instance, the couplet is a two line stanza, the triplet, a three line stanza, a quatrain is a four line stanza. There are also sestets (six lines), septets (seven lines) and octaves (eight lines).

verse— a line of traditional poetry written in meter. In addition, verse has a name depending upon the number of feet (see *foot*) per line: one foot (monometer), two feet (dimeter), three feet (trimeter), four feet (tetrameter), five feet (pentameter), six feet (hexameter), seven feet (heptameter), eight feet (octometer).

Traditional Poetry

You have probably seen more traditional poetry than any other kind. Traditional poetry follows certain patterns of rhyme and rhythm. Often, traditional poetry is arranged into a rhyme scheme. Look at the rhyme scheme of this poem by Lewis Carroll. The lines that rhyme are marked with the same letter.

How Doth the Little Crocodile

How doth the little crocodile	a
Improve his shining tail,	b
And pour the waters of the Nile	a
On every golden scale!	b
How cheerfully he seems to grin,	c
How neatly spreads his claws,	d
And welcomes little fishes in,	c
With gently smiling jaws!	d

Meter is another important pattern in traditional poetry. Meter is the rhythm you hear when a poem is read aloud. Clap while you read the poem about the crocodile. Can you feel the rhythm? The meter of a poem is made up of accented syllables and unaccented syllables. Clap on the accented syllables and don't clap on the unaccented syllables. Look at the nursery rhyme below. The syllables are marked so you can see the meter. An unaccented syllable is marked with ˘. An accented syllable is marked with ˘.

Pétĕr, Pétĕr, púmpkĭn éatĕr,

Hád ă wífe ănd cóuldn̆'t kéep hĕr;

Pút hĕr ín ă púmpkĭn shéll

Ănd thére hĕ képt hĕr vérў wéll.

Read it again. Clap when you come to an accented syllable (ˊ) and open your hands when you come to an unaccented syllable (˘).

Now try this one. Clap the rhythm while you read the nursery rhyme below. When you think you know what the meter is, mark the unaccented and accented syllables.

Georgie Porgie, pudding and pie,
Kissed the girls and made them cry;
When the boys came out to play,
Georgie Porgie ran away.

Extension: Read the crocodile poem aloud and mark the syllables as accented or unaccented.

Traditional Poetry *(cont.)*

In addition to rhyme and meter, traditional poetry has certain forms. Some forms of poetry have been around since before the printing press. Before people could buy a newspaper, there were messengers who went from town to town, sharing the news in the form of poetry, songs, and stories.

The Ballad

One of the earlier forms of poetry was the ballad. A ballad is a poem that tells a story. Ballads are usually written in quatrains (stanzas with four lines). They are generally quite lengthy, with many stanzas. Here is an example of two stanzas from a ballad titled "Ballad of Sir Patrick Spens" (it is about brave sailors on a ship that sank near the coast of Scotland):

> *They had not sailed a league, a league,*
> *A league but barely three,*
> *When the lift grew dark, and the wind blew loud,*
> *And gurly grew the sea.*
> *O long, long may the ladies sit,*
> *With their fans into their hand*
> *Before they see Sir Patrick Spens*
> *Come sailing to the strand!*

Here is an example from one stanza from a ballad written by a student of today.

> *My father's gone to New York state*
> *For business he must do.*
> *I wish that he were here with me,*
> *To taste this yummy stew.*
> *When he gets back, he promised me,*
> *A baseball game to see.*
> *If I but finish all my work,*
> *We'll see a game or three!*

Blank Verse

Blank verse does not rhyme, but it does have meter. Usually each line in blank verse has ten syllables. The first syllable is often unaccented and the second is accented. After that, every other syllable is accented. Here is an example of a student's blank verse:

> I took a ride upon a horse, and he
> was kind to me, through brambles and the wind
> we rode 'till nothing bothered me at last.

Extension: Share some news with a friend or family member in the form of a ballad. Write about an experience in blank verse. Is it more difficult or easier than you expected?

Traditional Poetry *(cont.)*

Cinquain

A cinquain poem always has five lines. Here is the structure of a cinquain poem:

Line 1-Title *(one noun)*
Line 2-Description of title *(two adjectives)*
Line 3-An action about the title *(three verbs)*
Line 4-A feeling about the title *(a four-word phrase)*
Line 5-Another word for the title *(one-word synonym)*.

Here is an example of a cinquain:

> Friskie
> Fuzzy, cuddly
> Wiggling, running, licking
> Happy to see me!
> Dog

On another sheet of paper, finish this cinquain about school.

___School___. *(noun)*

_____, _____, *(two adjectives)*

_____, _____, _____*(three verbs)*

_____, _____, _____, _____

(four words expressing a feeling about school)

_____ *(another word for school)*

Couplet

A couplet is made up of two lines that rhyme. Here is an example:

Couplets are lines that always rhyme.
In pairs they're rhyming all the time.

On another sheet of paper, finish the couplets below.

A poem, a poem, I cannot write
I tried and tried all through the _____

Through the door I tossed the ball
And watched it rolling down the _____

Up in the tree, I saw my cat
_____

Grasshopper, spiders and tiny ants
_____

Epic

An epic poem is a very long story poem about a hero or heroine and his or her adventures. An example of a famous epic poem is *The Odyssey* by Homer. It is about Odysseus, the Greek hero, and his adventures.

Extension: Write a cinquain or a few couplets. Make into a book and illustrate.

Traditional Poetry *(cont.)*

Free Verse

Free verse is poetry that does not have a regular meter and does not contain rhyme. It is different from blank verse because blank verse has meter and a certain number of syllables. Here are some examples of free verse:

Fog

The fog comes
on little cat feet.
It sits looking

over harbor and city
on silent haunches
and then moves on.

–Carl Sandburg

Rotting

Candy makes your teeth rot
TV makes your brain rot
Air makes the salad rot
Time makes the fruit rot

And hate makes your heart rot.

–Kiera Null, at age 11

Seeds . . . Creativity

Countless seeds
On the wind.
Slip into mystery,
Follow nature's gentle guidance
To spread, fly, swim,
Then burrow

In darkness.
And a few seeds grow
In the silence.
Even fewer continue to develop . . .
Fruit, Infant
Idea, Art.

–Kathleen "Casey" Null

(Originally published in *Where Are We Going Besides Crazy?*, copyright 1989, Bookcraft, Inc.)

Are you getting the idea? Now try writing a free verse about a butterfly.

Haiku

Haiku is a form of Japanese poetry that has three lines and is usually about nature. (See pages 28 and 29 for detailed descriptions and activities for this form).

Extension: Prepare a notebook to be used just for collecting poetry. With your notebook, go to the library and look through the poetry books. Find some free verse poems you like and copy them into your notebook. Illustrate the pages. Add more whenever you find a new one that you like. Add some that you've written yourself.

Traditional Poetry *(cont.)*

Limerick

A limerick is a traditional form of humorous verse with five lines. The rhyme scheme is a-a-b-b-a. Lines 1, 2 and 5, have 3 stresses. Lines 3 and 4 have 2. This may sound complicated, but once you read a few, you'll understand. Read these aloud so you can get a sense of the rhythm.

There was an Old Man with a beard,
Who said, "It is just as I feared!
Two Owls and a Hen,
Four Larks and a Wren,
Have all built their nests in my beard."

—*Edward Lear*

There once was a young man named Andy
Who always dressed up fine and dandy,
But walking one day,
He slipped by the bay,
And came home all battered and sandy.

There once was a young man named Jason
Who was told that he really must hasten.
While washing his clothes,
He stepped on his toes
And fell with a splash in the basin.

There once was a teacher named Gray,
Who said to his students one day,
"Now, you have until one,
Get a limerick done."
The class groaned the hour away!

Now try a limerick of your own. Start by brainstorming some lists of rhyming words. Circle those that you think might go together to make a funny limerick. Fill in the lines below (note the rhyming pattern at the end of each line).

_____ a

_____ a

_____ b

_____ b

_____ a

Lyric

Many people have written lyrics. Maybe you have, too. A lyric is simply a short poem that expresses a personal feeling with a musical rhythm. Here is an example of a lyric poem by William Wordsworth.

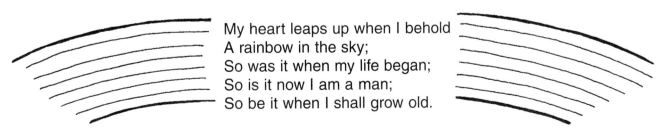

My heart leaps up when I behold
A rainbow in the sky;
So was it when my life began;
So is it now I am a man;
So be it when I shall grow old.

Extension: Write a limerick about someone you know. Try to use traits or actual events about that person in your limerick. If you have a friend who loves cats, your limerick can be about all of his or her cats. Illustrate your limerick and give it as a gift.

Traditional Poetry *(cont.)*

Sonnet

A sonnet is a poem with fourteen lines. It expresses the author's feelings. The poet best known for writing sonnets is Shakespeare, and the form most often used is known as the Shakespearian sonnet. A sonnet is the best form of poetry for expressing romantic or deep feelings.

Each line in the sonnet has ten syllables and every other syllable is stressed, beginning with the second syllable. The sonnet is three quatrains and a couplet. Sonnets usually present a problem in the first two quatrains. In the third quatrain, the poet begins to answer the problem and, in the final couplet, tries to solve the problem.

Here is a sonnet written by Shakespeare. Don't try to understand every word he writes. Shakespeare's poems must be read many times. Each time the sonnet is read, it is understood a little bit better. (The letters represent the structure of the sonnet.)

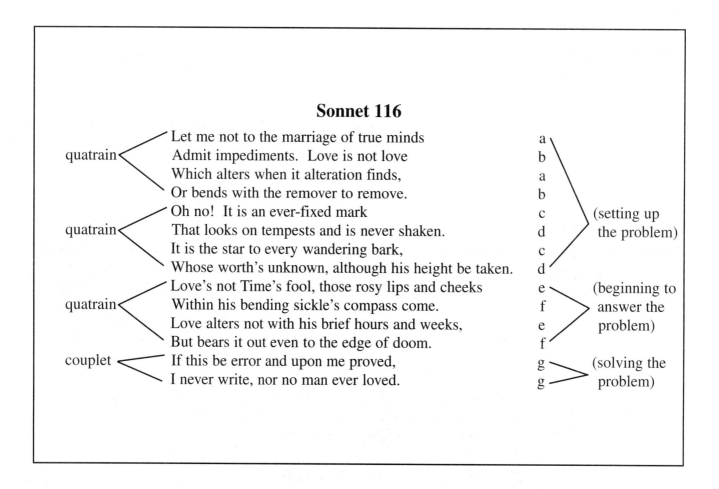

Sonnet 116

quatrain	Let me not to the marriage of true minds	a
	Admit impediments. Love is not love	b
	Which alters when it alteration finds,	a
	Or bends with the remover to remove.	b
quatrain	Oh no! It is an ever-fixed mark	c
	That looks on tempests and is never shaken.	d
	It is the star to every wandering bark,	c
	Whose worth's unknown, although his height be taken.	d
quatrain	Love's not Time's fool, those rosy lips and cheeks	e
	Within his bending sickle's compass come.	f
	Love alters not with his brief hours and weeks,	e
	But bears it out even to the edge of doom.	f
couplet	If this be error and upon me proved,	g
	I never write, nor no man ever loved.	g

(setting up the problem)

(beginning to answer the problem)

(solving the problem)

Extension: Choose a topic and try to write a Shakespearian sonnet. Don't be discouraged if it is difficult. Simply trying to write a sonnet deserves a pat on the back! Your attempt will really strengthen your poetic muscles.

Invented Poetry

Invented poetry is written in a form that you invent yourself. You can choose one of these forms invented by others or try something new.

Alphabet Poetry

Alphabet poetry uses a part of the alphabet to write a poem. To write one, choose the part of the alphabet that you want to use (5–10 letters) and write the letters, in order, down the left side of your paper. Then fill in the lines. Here are some examples:

Angry	Highly happy and
Babies	Ignorant ice cream eating
Come	Janitors and clerks
Down	Kick tin cans all the way to
Every	Luxembourg just to
Friday	Make an impression on
	Nice,
	Old fashioned, orangutans

Concrete Poetry

Concrete poetry is poetry written in a shape or design to match the meaning or feeling of the poem.

Headline Poetry

Headline poetry uses the words and phrases already created by newspaper editors. To create a headline poem, get a newspaper and read the headlines. Cut them out and apart and rearrange them on your paper to make a collage poem. Or you can simply write the combinations of words you want to use. Here is one:

Extension: Try writing an alphabet poem with all 26 letters of the alphabet. Write them on cutout shapes. For instance, on a blue star shape write a poem in silvery or white ink about stars.

Invented Poetry *(cont.)*

List Poetry

List poems use repetition as their structure. They are also a kind of comparison or a paying attention to small details we might not always notice. Here are a couple of list poems to give you the idea:

Houses

I see houses everywhere
There are houses to start out in
Houses to grow in
Houses to be sick in
Houses to hide in
Houses to be born in
Houses to die in . . .

I went out today
into the crowd
There were people smoking
and shoving and snarling
There were people rushing
and rustling and rendezvousing
There were people fearing
and fainting and following
There were people wondering why.

Name Poem

A name poem is just like an acrostic poem (see Name Poem activity on page 27), but it always uses a name. All you need to do is write the name down the left side of your paper and then fill in the lines with things about that person. Here is one:

Dares to dive in deep, dark pools
Easy with a laugh
Buys too many bubble wands
Best at baking bread
Into ice cream in a bowl
Every song is known by heart

Riddle Poetry

A riddle poem will have your reader guessing the subject of your poem. Here are examples; can you guess their subjects?

Thirty white horses upon a red hill,
Now they tramp, now they champ,
Now they stand still.

(answer: teeth and gums)

Four stiff-standers,
Four dilly-danders,
Two lookers, two crookers,
And a long wiggle-waggle.

(answer: cow)

Extension: Make a list of all the things that happen in a house and write a list poem. Illustrate it with a drawing of your own house. Write a riddle poem and read it to a friend. Can he or she guess what the poem is about?

Invented Poetry *(cont.)*

Terse Verse

Terse verse is poetry that consists of just two words! The two words need to be a very clever way to say something else. Here are some examples to get you thinking:

Subject		Terse Verse
Drooping Flower	=	Lazy Daisy
Braces	=	Tin Grin
Planting Lots of Trees	=	Tree Spree
Halloween	=	Fright Night
Witch with Chicken Pox	=	Itchy Witchy
Fast Elevator	=	Swift Lift
Large Hole	=	Big Dig
Worms	=	Great Bait

Phrase Poetry

A phrase poem defines the title of the poem with a list of phrases. Here is an example:

Swimming
Into the cold with a shock
slipping forward silently
bursting upward with a gasp
eyes stinging, blinking
floating soundlessly

Extension: Brainstorm in teams to come up with as many two-word terse verse poems as you can. Make an illustrated class book full of your terse verse poems. Share the book with parents at open house and with other classes (especially younger students).

Write a list of one word poem subjects and cut them up so they are on separate pieces of paper. Put them into a box with those of your classmates. Mix them up and draw three (each classmate does the same). Write three phrase poems on the three subjects you select. Have a poetry reading session with your class.

Doodles

To write poetry, you need to be creative.

To be creative, you need to take a deep breath, relax your mind, and use your imagination.

One way to do this is by doodling and drawing. There are two doodles in the space below. Use your imagination to finish them. You can use each one as a separate drawing or combine them into one drawing. Make them into anything you want them to be.

Extension: Now that you've experienced creating something from doodles, you can play a game with your classmates. On a blank piece of paper, draw a doodle. Pass it to your partner. Your partner makes your doodle into a drawing of something. Then, he or she makes a doodle for you. Continue to take turns and be as creative as you can.

Other ways to doodle: Each student in the class draws a doodle on a piece of paper and writes his or her name on the back. The papers are collected, mixed up, and passed out to the class. You should get someone else's doodle. Turn it into a drawing. When everyone has finished, share the art. Ask the doodle creator if the final drawing is similar to what he or she imagined it would be.

Each student takes a sheet of paper and draws nine doodles. (This will be very challenging but just wait!). The papers are collected and then passed out so each student has another classmates' doodle page. You will have nine new doodles to challenge you. Will you make nine different drawings? Can you use all nine doodles in one drawing, or will you combine some and draw some separately? When everyone is finished, take turns describing your experience. Was it difficult? Did you have an idea about what your doodles might be when finished? Did the artist who finished your doodles surprise you?

I Feel As Silly As...

A good way to warm up creative muscles is to play with similes. A simile compares two different things. (See pages 22 and 23 for an exercise in metaphor and simile.)

Examples

"I feel as angry as a hornet's nest!"
"I feel as tired as a rag doll that's lost its stuffing."

Now you try some. Be as creative as you can.

I feel as limp as a(n) _____

I feel as happy as a(n) _____

I feel as strong as a(n) _____

I feel as silly as a(n) _____

I feel as sad as a(n) _____

I feel as angry as a(n) _____

I feel as excited as a(n) _____

I feel as frightened as a(n) _____

I feel as light as a(n) _____

I feel as grumpy as a(n) _____

I feel as slow as a(n) _____

I feel as hungry as a(n) _____

I feel as sleepy as a(n) _____

Extension: In a section of a notebook or folder, write some character descriptions using similes. For instance, you might draw a character at the top of the page and then describe the character. Here is an example: "She was as skinny as the painted line dividing the highway. Her hair was as mossy and clumped as seaweed. Her eyes were as brown as chocolate. She was as feisty as a bunch of seagulls fighting over an open bag of potato chips."

This Is the Moment

An important part of being creative is being observant. Often, we spend so much time thinking about what happened yesterday and about what might happen tomorrow that we don't even notice today. To be creative, we need to notice things. Here is a form that you can use right now and anytime. Make copies of the form and carry them with you so you can record your observations at different times and in different places. Do this exercise often to increase your ability to be observant.

Right now I am _____
(location)

I see _____ people _____
(how many)

_____
(describe one or two people)

I see _____

_____
(describe the setting)

I hear _____

_____

I smell _____

I can taste _____
(If you are not eating at the time, is there a particular taste in your mouth? Sour? Bitter? Sweet? Is there a smell that is strong enough to affect your taste buds?)

I can feel _____

_____
(Think of objects in the setting that you may be touching or that may be touching you such as grass, clothing, heat, cold, etc.)

Extension: Keep a notebook of observations and record at least one each day. If you wish, you can add one more thing to record such as how you are feeling at the time (sad, glad, mad, etc.), and/or how ⁀ers around you are feeling. In a public place, record observations of the people around you. Make ⁀ries about the people based on your observations.

Alliteration

Alliteration is when the beginning sounds in a line of verse sound the same. Here are some examples of alliteration: "green grasslands of Gotham," "creamy and crunchy," "she shrugs and shuffles," "silently slipping," "pease porridge hot, pease porridge cold, pease porridge in the pot . . . ."

Here is a way to write a poem with alliteration. Begin by choosing a favorite letter of the alphabet. When you have your letter, take out a piece of paper and brainstorm a list of words that begin with that letter. When you have at least twenty words (the more the better), decide what kind of poem you would like to write. Will it rhyme? Would you prefer to write in free verse? Maybe you'd like to write a limerick. Go ahead and write. You might decide to write free verse, but after you start, you may change your mind and write a rhyming poem. That's okay. Here is how one student did it, just to give you an idea. Susannah chose the letter "s."

Here is her list of words:

shiny	Saturday	silent	say	so
scarlet	sunshine	sound	see	scrambled
simple	swift	scratch	sigh	scribble
sad	swish	skinny	swoosh	something

Here is the poem she wrote:

> On Saturday, she silently
> Scribbled something in the sunshine
> And sighed as a swift swoosh
> Scrambled her shiny, simple sayings.

Extension: Write the letters of the alphabet on separate pieces of paper, mix them up, and randomly select one. Use whatever letter you chose to brainstorm and write an alliterative poem. Do this for as many letters as you can. Divide a notebook into the letters of the alphabet. Collect interesting words and put them in the appropriate sections. When you write a poem, use your alliteration notebook to find combinations of words you might want to use.

Simile and Metaphor

You can be more creative in your writing by using similes and metaphors. A simile is a way of comparing two things. The comparison is written with the words *like* or *as*. A metaphor describes by comparing one thing to another without using the words *like* or *as*.

Here are two similes:

I'm as sharp as a pin.

The cloud is as puffy as a cotton ball.

Finish the similes below.

1. The wet dog smelled like_____

_____

2. The ice was as slick as_____

Now, here is a poem which uses a simile:

That star is like a shiny light.
Twinkling in the darkest night.

Use a simile to write a short poem. It does not have to rhyme.

_____

_____

_____

_____

_____

_____

22

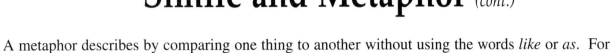

Simile and Metaphor *(cont.)*

A metaphor describes by comparing one thing to another without using the words *like* or *as*. For example:

The bird is a colorful rainbow.

I'm an accident waiting to happen.

Complete the metaphors below.

1. The child was a _____.

2. The star was a_____.

Use comparison words to complete these metaphors.

1. The cloud is a _____.

2. The tree is a _____.

3. The eagle is_____.

4. The ice was _____.

5. The moon was_____.

6. The wolf was _____.

7. The rain is _____.

8. The rock is_____.

Rhyme Time

You're a poet, but do you know it? Whenever you use words that sound alike, you are rhyming. Choose words from the word bank that rhyme with or sound like the words in the box.

bake	flop	playground	late

Word Bank

ate	merry-go-round	hound	gumdrop
found	great	bait	around
drop	fake	awake	skate
ache	bookshop	high top	create
snowflake	greyhound	sound	lake
roommate	break	plate	stop
lollipop	pop	cupcake	campground

Write word pairs on the lines below (example: bake—ache)

_____   _____

_____   _____

_____   _____

_____   _____

_____   _____

_____   _____   _____

_____   _____   _____

_____   _____   _____

Extension: Add more rhyming words to the lists. Write a poem when you find some rhymes you like.

Rhyming Shapes

Can you think of rhymes to go into the shapes on this page? Say the word on each shape and think of as many rhyming words as you can. Write them inside the shapes.

Extension: Make your own rhyming dictionary. Divide the pages of a notebook and allow two to four pages for each letter of the alphabet (you may prefer to use only one page for such letters as "x" or "u"). Begin by choosing a word to represent each letter of the alphabet: A-Act, B-Bat, C-Cat, etc. Then, on each page, make as many rhymes as you can with the word on the page. Write them in alphabetical order, for example: Bat—at, bat, cat, fat, flat, hat, mat, pat, rat, sat, splat, vat, etc. Once you get the hang of it, try to find rhymes for more challenging words such as banana or aquarium.

Couplets

A couple of apples is how many? Two apples! A couplet in poetry is two lines that rhyme.

Here are some rhyming pairs. See if you can write couplets using the rhymes. The first two are examples for you.

(Peas, Sneeze)

I don't like broccoli, squash, or peas,
And this is why, they make me sneeze!

(Fancy, Antsy)

Ruffles, bows, and anything fancy,
Are clothes that always make me antsy!

(Bunny, Funny)

_____

_____

(Flat, Splat)

_____

_____

(Jump, Clump)

_____

_____

(Dewy, Chewy)

_____

_____

(Worm, Squirm)

_____

_____

Extension: Make a class big book by having each student write a couplet about him or herself and illustrate it. Put them all together and share the book with parents and other classes.

Name Poem

You can write a poem by using a word and taking each letter of that word to begin a different line in your poem. This is called an acrostic poem.

Example for the word "cat":

Creeping' round the bed
Attacking my feet
Time to go outside

Now it's time to take your name
And write it in a row.
Make it fun, it's like a game
Every word will show.

Parts of you that you can share
On all the things you do
Even all that you would dare
Much to say' bout you!

Write each letter of your name in a box below and then write a name poem about yourself. It doesn't have to rhyme. Use the back of the page if your name has more than 10 letters.

Extension: Write a name poem for a friend. Add a picture and give it as a gift. If you want a challenge, see if you can make a rhyming name poem.

Haiku

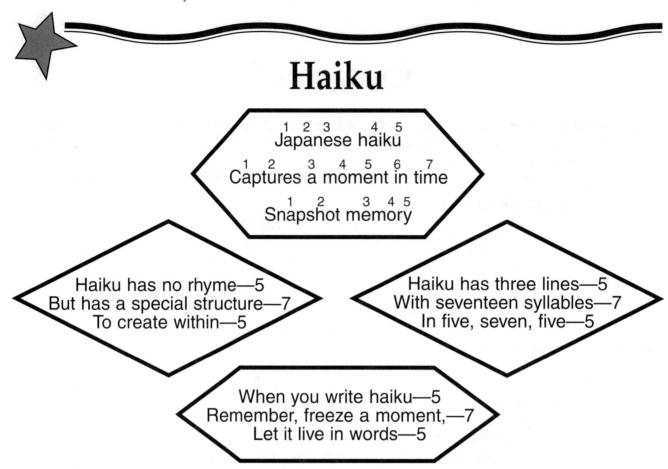

1 2 3   4 5
Japanese haiku

1 2   3 4 5   6   7
Captures a moment in time

1   2   3 4 5
Snapshot memory

Haiku has no rhyme—5
But has a special structure—7
To create within—5

Haiku has three lines—5
With seventeen syllables—7
In five, seven, five—5

When you write haiku—5
Remember, freeze a moment,—7
Let it live in words—5

Haiku is a form of Japanese poetry, usually about nature. The first line has five syllables, the second line has seven syllables, and the third line has five. Count the syllables in the haiku lines above.

Here are some examples of haiku:

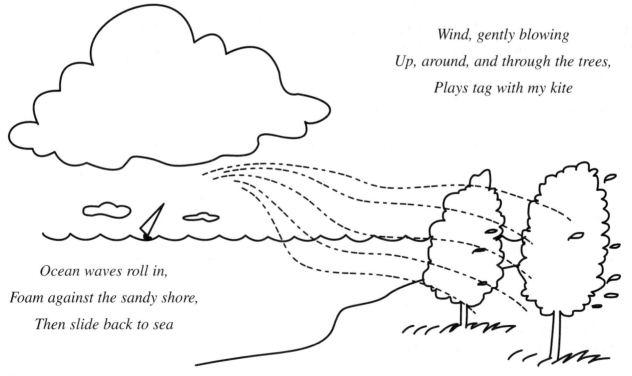

Wind, gently blowing

Up, around, and through the trees,

Plays tag with my kite

Ocean waves roll in,

Foam against the sandy shore,

Then slide back to sea

Haiku *(cont.)*

Now it's your turn to write haiku! Remember to count the syllables carefully. Begin by brainstorming. List all the words you can think of to describe "summer" and how you feel about it. Use some of your words to finish this haiku about summer.

<table>
<tr><td colspan="2">Summer Words</td></tr>
<tr><td>_____</td><td>_____</td></tr>
<tr><td>_____</td><td>_____</td></tr>
<tr><td>_____</td><td>_____</td></tr>
<tr><td>_____</td><td>_____</td></tr>
</table>

Your Poem

The bright sun shines on   —5

_____—7

_____—5

Now list all the words you can think of to describe winter and then write a winter haiku poem.

<table>
<tr><td colspan="2">Winter Words</td></tr>
<tr><td>_____</td><td>_____</td></tr>
<tr><td>_____</td><td>_____</td></tr>
<tr><td>_____</td><td>_____</td></tr>
<tr><td>_____</td><td>_____</td></tr>
</table>

Your Poem

_____—5

_____—7

_____—5

Are you getting the idea? On a separate piece of paper, choose a topic and brainstorm some words related to that topic. When you have enough words, choose your favorites and use them in a haiku in the space below.

_____

_____

_____

_____

_____

_____

Extension: Create haiku poems to give as gifts to friends and family members. You can write them on bookmarks, watercolored paper, special-colored paper, etc.

Free Verse

Free Verse
Is poetry without rhyme
And no form to hold you in.
You are set free to soar
And create snapshots and
Beautiful pictures to share.
Let your feelings flow,
Freely, poetically, and meaningfully,
Perfect,
Just the way it is.

While you don't need to worry about rhyme or meter with free verse, it is important to think about poetic expression. How do the words sound? Is there a flow? Use the senses, alliteration, simile, and metaphor, etc. to make your free verse poem special. Try to find ways to convey feelings in as few, carefully chosen words as possible.

Write a free verse poem about a member of your family.

_____

_____

_____

Write a free verse poem about a feeling.

_____

_____

_____

Write a free verse poem about a favorite place.

_____

_____

_____

Extension: Use a notebook to record a daily free-verse. Write each day about a feeling, an observation, a person or an experience. Illustrate if you like.

Limerick

A limerick is a five-line poem with a rhyme scheme of a-a-b-b-a. Some think that the limerick began in Limerick, Ireland. Others are certain that Shakespeare originated the limerick. However it began, the limerick always has a humorous tone. Limericks became very popular when Edward Lear wrote two books, *The Book of Nonsense* and *More Nonsense*. Lear writes limericks in the older form, which uses the same word at the end of the first and the last lines. Here is an example of a limerick by Edward Lear:

> A flea and a fly in a flue
> Were imprisoned, so what could they do?
> Said the flea, "Let us fly!"
> Said the fly, "Let us flee!"
> So they flew through a flaw in the flue.

Do you notice the alliteration in this limerick? The word flue is repeated in the last line. More modern limericks do not use the same word for the end of the first and last lines. The words do rhyme, however. Here's a funny example:

> There once was a young man from Kew
> Who found a dead mouse in his stew.
> Said the waiter, "Don't shout
> Or wave it about,
> Or the rest will be wanting one too!"

Tap your foot while you read each limerick and notice the beat.

Finish the limerick below using the word bank for your ending rhymes.

Jason	Larry	Matthew	nose	see	bay	basin
clothes	carry	cashew	hasten	red	toes	hairy
dandy	said	he	chasten	berry	head	sews
handy	marry	day	Barry	"Achoo!"	Andy	candy

There once was a man named _____

Who_____

_____

_____

_____

Extension: Use the word bank above to make more limericks. How many can you write?

Quatrain

A quatrain is not some strange train that is taken to the land of Qua. "Quatr" means four, and a quatrain has four lines with a rhyming pattern of a-a-b-b, a-b-a-b, a-a-a-a, or a-b-c-d. The last two are often used in long poems so that there is a pattern among all the quatrains. This is one of the most common forms of poetry. Here is an example of a quatrain from an old nursery rhyme titled "Tom, the Piper's Son."

> Tom, he was a piper's son,
> He learned to play when he was young,
> But all the tune that he could play
> Was "Over the hills and far away."

Do you see the a-a-b-b rhyming scheme? Tap your foot as you read it again. Do you feel the meter? Even the mean, giant ogre in "Jack and the Beanstalk" spoke in a quatrain:

> Fee, fi, fo, fum,
> I smell the blood of an Englishman,
> Be he alive, or be he dead
> I'll grind his bones to make my bread.

Using the four lines below, write a quatrain with the ending rhymes that are already written for you. It has a rhyming pattern of a-b-a-b.

_____celebrate

_____there

_____great

_____care

Now that you've written a quatrain, read it aloud while tapping out the rhythm. Do you need to make any changes? Make the changes you need so that it has a noticeable rhythm. Choose another rhyming pattern (a-a-b-b or a-a-a-a) and try another quatrain.

Extension: Get together with a friend and while you are walking, doing a chore, or just sitting and waiting, make up quatrains together. Take turns being the composer of the first line. When you or your friend come up with a first line, the other creates the second line, and so on until you have four lines. You might want to have a piece of paper handy in case you come up with some really good ones. Write a longer story poem of four or more quatrains.

Cinquain

A cinquain is a structured, five line poem. It always follows this pattern:

Line one–A one word title (*noun*)
Line two–Two words that describe the title (*adjectives*)
Line three–Three words that show the action of the title (*verbs*)
Line four–Four words that express a feeling about the title (*phrase*)
Line five–One word that is another word for the title (*synonym*)

Here is an example of one student's cinquain:

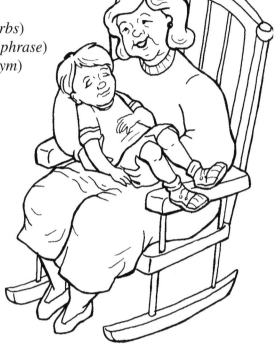

> Nanna
> Round, Soft
> Humming, Baking, Loving
> Her lap's for me
> Grandma

Choose a topic from the list and write a cinquain on a separate sheet of paper. Add art to illustrate your cinquain.

• grandma	• school	• vacation
• grandpa	• cookies	• summer
• baby	• mom	• Thanksgiving
• wind	• dad	• science
• snow	• friend	• pet

Extension: Teach cinquain writing to a younger group of students. You may need to explain nouns, adjectives, verbs, and synonyms, so be patient. Be sure they illustrate their cinquains. Write a cinquain about a family member and illustrate it or mount it on colored cardboard or construction paper. Give it as a gift.

Diamante

Are you ready for the challenge of a diamante poem? *Dia* in this use means opposite. This is a structured poem that can be a little challenging. Let's begin with an example:

1.   **Puppy**
2.   **Pudgy, Bouncy**
3.   **Wiggling, Chewing, Squealing**
4.   **Soft, Fat tummy, Tall, Lean**
5.   **Sleeping, Barking, Hunting**
6.   **Loyal, Patient**
7.   **Dog**

A diamante has seven lines.
    Lines 1 and 7 state subjects that are opposites (puppy/dog).
    Line 2 contains two adjectives describing the subject of line 1.
    Line 3 contains three action words specific to the subject of line 1.
    Line 4 contains four adjectives. The first two describe the subject in line 1 and the second two
        describe the subject in line 7.
    Line 5 contains three action words specific to the subject of line 7.
    Line 6 contains two adjectives describing the subject of line 7.

For your first diamante, choose a pair of opposites from the word bank. Write your poem on a separate sheet of paper. When you have it the way you want it, write it on the seven lines below.

Head-Foot	Mom-Dad	Villain-Hero	Tadpole-Frog
Flower-Weed	Night-Day	Summer-Winter	Friend-Enemy
Old-Young	Shoes-Barefoot	Cold-Hot	Dog-Cat

_____

_____

_____

_____

_____

_____

_____

Extension: Think of a diamante as a way to write a report. If you are studying historical figures, use a diamante to describe two who were opposites. For a book report, write another diamante about two opposite characters in a book.

Clerihew

A clerihew is a short, usually humorous, and light poem about a famous person whose name makes up the first line. It was invented by Edmund Clerihew. The form for this poem is two couplets (four lines with the rhyme scheme of a-a-b-b). Here are some examples:

Sir James Jeans
Always says what he means;
He is really perfectly serious
About the Universe being Mysterious.

The thing we like 'bout Henry Ford
Is he didn't let himself get bored.
He thought of making cars for us
When they break down, we take the bus.

Think of someone in history who you have been studying. Write a clerihew about him or her. Can you make it light hearted or humorous? Remember the a-a-b-b rhyme scheme.

Write your clerihew in the box below. Draw a portrait of the subject beside it.

Extension: Have a poetry reading in class where everyone reads his or her clerihew about a person in history. Afterwards, put them all in a book to share at open house. Write a humorous clerihew about someone you know in your life today.

Word-List Poem

Your teacher will give you the opportunity to reach into a basket or box and take a "pinch" of words. Reach in and take a few of the word slips. While other students are "pinching" their words, write yours in the box below.

Now that you have written them down, you can allow your teacher to collect the slips. Look at your words. Can you find any relationships among them? It may be difficult, but use your imagination. You can do it.

Now you can make a word web. Decide which word in your box will be the theme of your web and write it in the center circle of the web. The words you write in the other circles should relate to the theme. Think about how the other words fit with the theme and write them in the outer circles. Fill in the rest of the circles with any other words you wish.

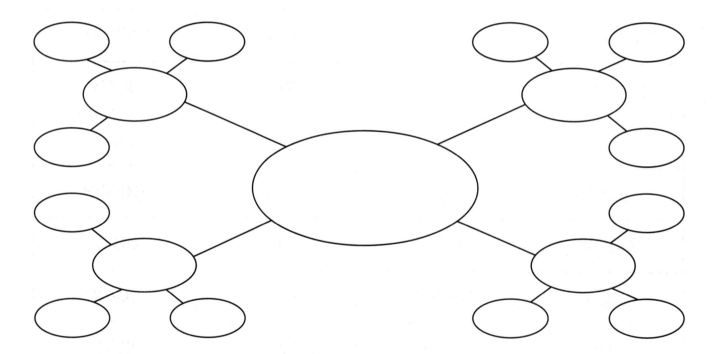

After brainstorming and completing your web, take a piece of paper and, using the words you pinched, write a poem. You can write any kind of poem you would like. You don't have to use every word you thought of, but you should use all of the words you "pinched."

Extension: Illustrate your poem. You can also use "pinched" words to write a creative story. To make it easier, choose only two or three words. To make it more challenging, choose more words.

Word-List Poem *(cont.)*

Teacher Note: Make five to ten copies of this page and cut the words on each page apart into their own empty box. Divide your class by the number of boxes. Each group of students will have a complete set of words without duplicates.

baseball	spider	ice cream	impossible
vacation	tornado	grandparents	bird
laugh	monster	bubbles	sing
sneeze	sneakers	peanuts	toy
telephone	giggle	corncob	balloon
pancake	dog	stripes	party
hopscotch	clouds	elephant	skips
pizza	caboose	snow	gorilla
purple	daffodil	rainbow	book
moon	cookies	mud	bottle
music	river	mountain	wagon
rain	huge	shell	quicksand
light	snow	plums	gallop

Personal Poem

This is a project your family is sure to enjoy. To create it, you will need the following:

- a sheet of medium-weight drawing paper, about 14" x 11" (36 cm x 28 cm)
- a photograph of yourself that measures about 4" x 6" (10 cm x 15 cm)
- pencils, pens, markers, or crayons
- the Personal Poem form (page 39)

What is a personal poem? Read the example below.

Jason
Affectionate, Shy, Athletic
Sibling of
Michael, Chris, Kiera
Lover of
Soft, warm, furry pets, rainy days,
Cool Pools
Who feels
love, Affection, Kindness
Who needs
Affection, understanding, generosity
Who gives
love, friendship, affection
Who fears
large waves, darkness, unknown things
Who would like to see
The tops of clouds, the ground from above
the blackness of space.
Buffington

After writing your poem on a practice paper, glue your photograph to the drawing paper and write your poem beside it. Use fancy letters for your first and last names. Use markers or crayons to add art in the leftover spaces on the paper.

Personal Poem *(cont.)*

To begin, fill in the following blanks:

_____

First name

_____ , _____ , _____ ,

List three adjectives about yourself

Sibling (or child/ grandchild) of

_____

Lover of

_____

Who feels

_____

Who needs

_____

Who gives

_____

Who fears

_____

Who would like to see

_____

_____

Last name

(The example on page 38 will give you more ideas.)

Animal Poem

Look at the animal outlines below. Think of words that rhyme with each one. Write your list in the box beside the outline and write the poem inside the outline.

Example:

Rhyming Cat Words

cat	hat
fat	flat
sat	

My cat is fat
and sat on my hat.
It's flat!

Rhyming Bunny Words

_____ _____

_____ _____

_____ _____

Rhyming Pig Words

_____ _____

_____ _____

_____ _____

Rhyming Snake Words

_____ _____

_____ _____

_____ _____

Extension: Draw a large outline of your favorite animal and write a poem on its shape. Can you find rhyming words for horse, puppy, cow, lamb, whale, or even hamster?

Holiday Poem

Take a piece of blank paper and write a holiday poem about a special day. The poem will have seven lines.

Line 1–Name of the holiday
Line 2–Something you see on this holiday
Line 3–Something you smell on this holiday
Line 4–Something you hear on this holiday
Line 5–Something you taste on this holiday
Line 6–Something you touch on this holiday
Line 7–Name of the holiday

Draw a picture to go with your poem.

Examples:

Fourth of July
Red, White, and Blue
Smoky Barbecues
Booming, Clapping Fireworks
Juicy, Slippery Watermelon
Stinging Sparklers
Fourth of July

Halloween
Glowing Jack-o'-Lanterns
Freshly cut Pumpkin
Children giggling, "Trick or treat!"
Sweet, candy corn
Scratchy costumes
Halloween

Extension: On a large sheet of construction paper, write your poem and decorate the page with a border of art. (For example, Jack-o'-Lanterns and bats could be used for a border of a Halloween poem.) Have your teacher laminate your finished project to make a place mat for your holiday dinner! Make several, different poem place mats for your entire family.

Roses-Are-Red Greetings

You are going to make something for a favorite person: a poem on a greeting card. Begin with the traditional "Roses-Are-Red" poem, and brainstorm as many variations as you can. Try finishing the poems below. Then, take another piece of paper and write some more.

Roses are red,
Violets are blue,
Believe it or not,
I made this for you!

Roses are red,
Violets are blue,

_____

_____

Roses are red,
Violets are blue,

_____

_____

In your poems, roses don't always need to be red, and violets don't have to be blue. Roses can be pink, striped yellow, white or any color you wish. Violets can be purple, aqua, navy, blue-green, or lavender.

Example:

Roses are red,
Violets are navy,
Your hair is pretty,
'Cause it's so wavy.

Roses are_____ ,

Violets are _____ ,

_____

_____

Keep trying. Choose one of your poems and write it on the front of a greeting card.

Roses-are-Red Greetings *(cont.)*

To make a poetry greeting card you will need:

one sheet of 9" x 11" (23 cm x 28 cm) paper (Light colors work best.)

markers, crayons, pens, pencils

1. Fold your paper in half.

2. Fold it in half again.

3. Your card now has four surfaces (front, back, and two inside) on which to write and draw.

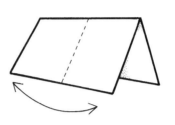

Look at your card and decide which will be the front, the inside, and the back.

On the front of your card you will write the first two lines of your poem. On the inside of your card, write the last two lines of your poem.

Front

Inside

Roses are red,
Violets are blue,

Believe it or not,
I made this for you!

Happy Birthday, Grandpa!
Love,
Christopher

Add art and a personal message such as one of the following:

Happy Anniversary, Mom and Dad
Love, Josette

I Miss You!
Good Luck

On the back of your card, give yourself credit as poet and artist with a sentence such as, "Poem and art by the one and only _____."
                    your name

Extension: Plan ahead to decorate your card with dried rose petals. Place the petals between newspaper and press them beneath heavy books for 4–6 weeks. When you make your Roses-Are-Red card, fasten the petals to the card with a few drops of glue. Draw a stem using a marker or crayon. You can also create tissue-paper roses, tie them into a bouquet and attach your card to them to make a spectacular gift for someone special.

Feelings Poem

Many poems are about feelings. In some poems you can feel the mood when you read them. Before you write one of these poems, think about different feelings and describe them.

Example:

When I am feeling happy, I...

feel like I am full of warm, delicious air that is rising and making me feel lighter and I want to smile at everyone and I giggle a lot and want to run and I can hear birds and see blue sky and tell everyone to join me.

When I am feeling sad, I...

_____

_____

_____

_____

When I am feeling lonely, I...

_____

_____

_____

_____

When I am feeling afraid, I...

_____

_____

_____

_____

When I am feeling angry, I...

_____

_____

_____

_____

Choose your favorite to write a feelings poem. One of your writings may already be a poem! Remember, a poem doesn't always have to rhyme.

Extension: Keep a feelings journal. In a notebook, title different sections with headings such as angry, frustrated, annoyed, sad, etc. When you are having strong feelings, open your journal and write about them.

Feelings Poem *(cont.)*

There are many ways to write a poem about your feelings. Here are some ways to get started.

An acrostic poem might look like this:

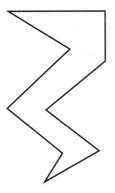

All alone in a big place
Following strangers
Ready to cry
Alone, alone
I wish I were home
Danger is everywhere!

Spell the feeling word down the left side of a paper and then complete the poem.

Another way to write a feelings poem is to write the feeling word on the first line and then write a line describing that feeling using each of your five senses (seeing, hearing, tasting, touching, and smelling). Here is an example:

Embarrassed
Kim and Chris are looking at me,
I hear people laughing and joking,
My mouth feels like it is full of dusty moths,
My skin feels all prickly and my ears are burning,
I start to smell sweat,
I am so embarrassed!

Extension: Try writing a poem without naming the feeling. Write it in any form you wish. See if your classmates can guess the feeling. Here is an example; can you guess the feeling?

The clouds get thicker
And darker
They bump into each other
And crash, groan, and shout
Soon they are one, big slab of gray
Covering all the blue of the sky
Pressing down on me.
(Feeling: Anger)

More Poetry Ideas

Mud Poem

What do you think of mud? Do you like it or hate it? Do you think it's fun to play in the mud? Have you ever had a mud fight or made a mud pie? Did mud ever get you in trouble? Did it ever ruin your shoes? How does it feel when it squishes between your toes?

Write a poem about mud. Use words such as puddle, squishy, mud pie, slimy, gooey, slippery, messy, barefoot, toes, stomp, splatter, wiggle, wet, cool, and damp.

Use what you have learned about writing poetry and choose your favorite style to write your mud poem. Use a separate sheet of paper and illustrate your poem.

Poetry by the Numbers

Take a blank sheet of paper and write a poem with the first line having one word, the second line with two words, the third line with three words, the fourth with four words and the fifth with five words. For example:

Tree
Trembling leaves
Shimmer at sunset
The trunk is solid
The roots reach for me.

Create a Class Poetry Magazine

Write lots of poems. Select one or more of your favorites to submit to your teacher for a class publication. Be sure your poems are easy to read and have been checked for spelling errors. Your teacher will collect poetry from each student and assign specific jobs such as editors, artists, typists (if needed), layout artists, etc.

If you are an editor, your job will be to check the poems for legibility and spelling. Check with the poet before you make any changes. Poetry is very creative, and there may be intentional capitalization or unusual grammatical usage. The editor will also organize the poems, and if there are many of them, he or she may decide to have sections and give each section a title.

If you are a layout artist, you will decide how and where to place each poem on the page. You will also decide where to place art and may make suggestions to the artists. As an artist, your job will be to create art to illustrate the poetry magazine. Editors and layout artists will make suggestions or give you assignments such as "Make some kind of floral border around the poem on this page," or "Draw a cat to illustrate this poem." You may be given an assignment that is more difficult. You may be given a poem that doesn't suggest a particular piece of art. You may need to illustrate a mood or a feeling.

Your teacher will be the publisher of your magazine, so be sure he or she sees your work before it goes to press. When all of your pages are ready and you have them in order, you can make photocopies and bind your magazine. Give extra copies to your family, friends, another class, and the school library.

Congratulations, you are a poet. Now it's time to give your poetry a final edit. Place a poem in front of you and look it over with the following checklist:

Poetry Writing Checklist

After reviewing each section, make a check in the box.

☐ **Have you checked the title of your poem? Does it make sense and add something to your poem? Does it catch the reader's attention?**

☐ **Have you looked at the form of your poem? How does it look and how does it sound? Read it aloud to hear how it sounds. Even the way it is arranged on the page will add or detract from a reader's enjoyment.**

☐ **What about capitalization? In traditional poetry the first word of each line is capitalized. This is not always true with free verse. You may want to capitalize just a few of the words for emphasis.**

☐ **Is your poem clear? Will it be too difficult to understand? Is it complete? Did you leave anything out?**

☐ **Did you check your poem for spelling and punctuation? Does your poem flow? Do you need to rewrite any parts?**

☐ **Is your poem in meter? Does it have a rhythm you can sense? Try clapping or tapping a finger or foot while you read it aloud or silently.**

☐ **If your poem rhymes, do your rhymes work naturally? Do they sound right?**

☐ **Is your poem easy to read? Do you need to type it or rewrite it more carefully?**

Make your corrections or changes and you're ready to present your final copy!

Poetry Frames

After you have written your poems, copy them into the frames.

48